# THE PAINFUL POIGNANCY OF DESIRE

*An Introduction to Romantic and Postromantic Poetry*

Claudia Moscovici

University Press of America,® Inc.
Lanham · Boulder · New York · Toronto · Plymouth, UK

Copyright © 2007 by
University Press of America,® Inc.
4501 Forbes Boulevard
Suite 200
Lanham, Maryland 20706
UPA Acquisitions Department (301) 459-3366

Estover Road
Plymouth PL6 7PY
United Kingdom

All rights reserved
Printed in the United States of America
British Library Cataloging in Publication Information Available

Library of Congress Control Number: 2006934332
ISBN-13: 978-0-7618-3644-5 (paperback : alk. paper)
ISBN-10: 0-7618-3644-6 (paperback : alk. paper)

∞™ The paper used in this publication meets the minimum
requirements of American National Standard for Information
Sciences—Permanence of Paper for Printed Library Materials,
ANSI Z39.48—1984

# Contents

Acknowledgements

Introduction: Romanticism and human emotion     1

1    Romantic poetry: "The spontaneous overflow of powerful feelings"     5

2    Postromanticism: The art of passion     13

Bibliography     19

3    Postromantic poetry: The painful poignancy of desire     23

About the Author     89

# Acknowledgements

I would like to thank my parents, Henri and Elvira Moscovici, for giving me a collection of Mihai Eminescu's Romantic poetry as a gift for my eighth birthday and for encouraging my dreams ever since.

Many thanks to my husband, Dan Troyka, for being so loving and supportive of my aspirations. I would also like to express gratitude to Robbie, my mother in law, who is not only a good friend but also a patron of postromantic art. Many thanks to my friend Eolake for having seen promise in the postromantic movement and for being one of its patrons.

Thanks also to my children, Sophie and Alex, for being their lovely selves and so patient with me. Sophie is a young poet and artist in her own right. May she accomplish all of her artistic dreams.

Some of my love poems published in this book have also appeared in the following literary magazines: *Enigma Magazine*, *The Fairfield Review*, *WINGS*, *Nanny Fay Poetry Magazine*, *The Poetic Matrix*, *Three Cup Morning*, *Soul Fountain*, *Slate and Style* and *Möbius*.

I'm grateful to my partner in the postromantic movement, the sculptor Leonardo Pereznieto, for his unwavering ambition and collaboration and to the talented designer Jacques Tararan for creating our website, postromanticism.com, and well as for producing the image on the cover of this book. Thank you also to my good friends, Pascal Ifri, Eric Turcat, Dider Karolinski, John Isbell, Isabel Roche and Linda Robison for their friendship and encouragement.

*Introduction*

# Romanticism and human emotion

In his study of Romanticism, *The Mirror and the Lamp*, M. H. Abrams distinguishes between a theory and an orientation. A theory begins with a set of assumptions that lead to a conclusion which follows logically from them. Romanticism lacks the internal consistency and the rational structure of a theory. Nonetheless, the writing of the Romantics points to related ways of conveying human emotion. As Abrams explains referring to Wordsworth in particular, for the Romantics, "A work of art is essentially the internal made external, resulting from a creative process operating under the impulse of feeling, and embodying the combined product of the poet's perceptions, thoughts, and feelings" (22).

Clearly, Romanticism is not the expression of raw, subconscious impulses, as the Surrealists would later describe the automatism of their own art. If Abrams states that expressive Romantic theories comprise an orientation, it's because they present different ways of processing emotions thoughtfully for artistic ends. As literary critics often point out, the role of emotions differs vastly from author to author. Romantic texts engage intellectual history, leading us to wonder: is emotion visceral and uncontrollable, as so many thinkers, from Plato to Kant, had maintained? Is it related in some fundamental way to what we know about the world, as the Stoics postulated? Is it tied to our ethical beliefs and tendencies, as Hume and Rousseau claimed in their partial defenses of sympathy? Is it induced by art, as Wordsworth and Baudelaire would declare? The difference in assumptions about emotion and its role in artistic creation contributes to the richness and versatility of Romantic literature and to the expressive models of art that underpin it.

Romantic poetry and literature link emotion to artic expression in ways that engage the big questions of almost every field of what we now call the humanities and social sciences. Given the diversity and wide-ranging intellectual implications of Romanticism, it's difficult to limit it even to the boundaries of an orientation. Yet the question remains, so let's return to it: in what ways can we speak meaningfully of a Romantic orientation? Like Abrams, I believe that there is one, indeed. I think we're in a better position to understand Romanticism by looking at its philosophical underpinnings and seeing how radically it has transformed the way we look at emotion in general and at passion in particular. For Romanticism was the most significant movement in Western culture to render passion and its artistic expression not an object of fear or ambivalence, but rather a highly desirable quality; one which is indispensable to human happiness.

In *Upheavals of Thought*, Martha Nussbaum traces the most prominent philosophical arguments for and against emotion. The con side tends to win over the pro side. Nussbaum shows that even those philosophers who were generally sympathetic to emotions—including Aristotle, the Stoics, Smith and Rousseau—warned against their uncontrollable nature and the danger they posed to reason (in the pursuit of knowledge) and to ethics (in the pursuit of the good life). Rousseau and Hume make some apologies for emotion in their study of sympathy, but even they qualify extensively.

Nussbaum considers in particular the Kantian argument against the emotions, which was very influential during the Enlightenment and which the Romantics had to contend with. Kant argues that emotions are too subjective, unreliable and volatile to provide an adequate basis for moral conduct. To address this objection, Nussbaum breaks it down into its component parts. First, such an argument tells us that emotions can be dangerous because they focus upon the individual and his or her personal goals or projects rather than the good of humanity. Second, the argument goes, emotions are associated with extremely close and intense attachments that may be "too partial or unbalanced" to lead to ethical decisions. (12) Third, it's objected that even those emotions that we consider positive—such as love or compassion—are often inseparable from destructive emotions, such as jealousy, anger and hatred. Although Kant stated this argument most compellingly, many philosophers that Nussbaum examines in her book--including Plato, Aristotle, the Stoics, Descartes, Smith,

Rousseau, and Kant himself –attempt to prove in one way or another that emotions are uncontrollable and destructive impulses (much of the same order as our bodily drives) that are unreliable motivations for morality. (13)

To detach emotion from the ethical standards and rationalist assumptions that were so inhospitable to it, Romantic authors first aestheticized it. Emotion, they illustrate, is above all related to the way we create and appreciate art. It's not, as philosophers tended to argue, primarily related to how we regulate ourselves or respond ethically to other human beings. Most Romantics did not go so far as to say that art could never be judged by moral criteria. Even when the late-Romantic theory of "art for art's sake" became all the rage in France in the 1830's, art was still not regarded as immune to moral judgment. Nonetheless, the Romantics made it possible for us to see emotion as tied to creativity and meaning in a way that rendered moral responses secondary to aesthetic ones. Once they made this important shift in the link between art and ethical value, the Romantics could reconnect emotion to all other important human faculties--cognition, perception and rational thought--in new, refreshing and complex ways. Under their pens, emotion, and especially passion, became the center of human existence, its most exalted state and a conduit to beauty and meaning.

This book offers an introduction to Romantic and postromantic poetry by placing special emphasis upon passion, which is more than a Romantic theme; it's the Romantic ethos. For the past ten years I have taught general "arts and humanities" courses in philosophy, literature and the arts. My students have always asked a fundamental question which all teachers are obliged to address: why is this subject of the past--be it Neoclassicism, Romanticism, Modernism or whatever else--relevant and interesting to them?

The second and third parts of this book address such a question. By presenting aspects of the postromantic movement and including samples of my own postromantic poetry, I hope to illustrate that the Romantic movement is not only a significant part of literary history. Romanticism is still worth studying because it gave human beings, and can give our generation as well, pleasure, beauty and hope. It continues to awaken our emotions, stimulate our imaginations, stir our sensibilities and inspire art and poetry today.

*Part I*

# Romantic poetry:
# "The spontaneous overflow
# of powerful feelings"

Romanticism connected the sentiment of passionate love to artistic expression perhaps more closely than any other literary movement by describing both as the undistorted expression of intense and genuine emotion. Wordsworth's famous definition of poetry in the 1802 Preface to the *Lyrical Ballads* as "the spontaneous overflow of powerful feelings" applied not only to a new understanding of art, but also to a new understanding of human identity. In this succinct phrase, Wordsworth challenged Neoclassical assumptions about the role of the artist and of art, the kind of audience art should affect and the values it should propose.

Each word chosen by Wordsworth is significant. If poetry is spontaneous, then it no longer needs to be guided by the rigid codes of Neoclassical art. If it's an overflow springing from the artist's imagination, then the artist is the most important part of the poetic process, since he's the source of the overflow. If poetry expresses powerful feelings, then its representations of how feelings are produced and of their contexts--in nature as well as in emotional bonds of friendship or love--will affect how society perceives emotion. If the object of poetry is to express the poet's powerful feelings, then he or she is defined as someone with internal, psychological and emotive qualities rather than primarily in terms of his social position. If reality is conveyed through the poet's imagination--and transformed by the poetry--then what matters most is not how accurately the poet conveys that reality, but how he or she distills it through his or her style, rendering it evocative, interesting and moving. Literature and poetry become above all else an expression of human emotion, and that emotion connects the modern self to the artistic medium of expression.

Perhaps it is this causal link between art and human emotion that contributes both to the splendor of Romanticism and to its vulnerability. Modernist and postmodernist writers would attack precisely these intimate connections between human identity, emotions and their poetic and passionate expressions. They suggest that it's naïve and unfounded to assume that true emotions are the basis of human nature, that such a nature exists at all, that even if it exists, it can be communicated without distortion and, most importantly, that art should have anything to do with such lived experience. The Modernist valorization of women's fashion and of the dandy, for example, offers a striking example of the assumption that it may be, in fact, the artificial constructions of art that guide the conventions we assume to be natural in life. Once human identity becomes freed from our understanding of nature, the expression of emotion, poetic or not, can no longer make direct claims to sincerity and authenticity. The expression of emotion may be just rhetorical or imitative rather than conveying what we truly feel.

Yet should we be so thoroughly convinced of the way Modernism and postmodernism describe the connection between emotion and art as opposed to the models offered by Romanticism? Is the link between emotion and art necessarily unfounded and naïve? To begin exploring this question, I will examine briefly two bookmarks of the Romantic movements: Wordsworth's 1802 Preface to *The Lyrical Ballads*, the theoretical blueprint of Romanticism and excerpts from Baudelaire's *Salon de 1846*, which inaugurates the beginnings of modernity. In so doing, I will emphasize the relevance of Romantic aesthetics today, hinting at the hidden continuities between the Romantic movement and current intuitions about the connection between emotion and art.

In the Preface to the *Lyrical Ballads*, Wordsworth elaborates what would become known as the underlying premises of British Romanticism. Although not systematic enough to be called a theory or philosophy of Romanticism, and although it speaks primarily of Wordsworth's and Coleridge's own poetry, this preface nonetheless sets the tone, in an eloquent and thoughtful manner, for the vaster and diverse Romantic movements which would follow. Furthermore, if as readers seasoned by the postmodern critiques of Romanticism, we expect Wordsworth's aesthetics to be naïve, when reading the Preface we are pleasantly surprised. There's nothing simplistic about Wordsworth's model of artistic expression. At each step of describing the aesthetic process, Wordsworth is careful to emphasize its complexity. He does, indeed, mention not once, but twice that "all good poetry is the spontaneous overflow of powerful feelings," yet we must unpack this dense statement to see what it means. For not only does the author not assume art to spring directly from emotion, but also he does not conceive of its expression and impact upon readers in a naïve manner.

In the beginning of his essay, Wordsworth declares that "the principal object proposed myself in these Poems is to choose incidents and situations from common life" (392). His choice of subject is already original because it rejects the Neoclassical rule that poetry should focus primarily upon extraordinary events and characters. Wordsworth transforms not only the choice of subject of art, but also, and more fundamentally, the manner of its representation.

As we are aware, Neoclassical art had a mimetic orientation, in that it viewed art as an imitation of aspects of the universe. The key vehicle for this kind of imitation was visual: a picture was viewed as best approximating the object it imitated. Poetry was supposed to imitate painting by focusing upon visual imagery that produced a mental picture of the object it represented in the mind of the reader. Horace's *Ars Poetica*, written in the first century B.C., and particularly his phrase *ut pictura poesis*, was interpreted by seventeenth-century authors as establishing a parallel between the two arts. However, no matter how hard they artists tried and how they were, neither pictorial nor written art could perfectly reproduce its object. In fact, all that could be claimed was that the artistic representation was *like* its object, or an analogue of it.

As M. H. Abrams observes in *The Mirror and the Lamp*, Neoclassical defenders of art solved this problem (of the gap between image and reality) by arguing that art is not an imitation of nature, but rather a selective and improved representation of its real or ideal essence. The representation is not less than the object it is supposed to depict, but on the contrary, better: hence the French phrase, *la belle nature* or beautiful nature. The objects represented are improved by the artist's technique and craft, which are in turn perfected by the rules that governed his or her particular art form. In addition, the purpose of art as imitation was to elevate and instruct its readers: to please while also edifying them. Generally speaking, there are two kinds of objects represented by Neoclassical art: 1) objects of sense-perception (things we can see); and 2) objects of thought, such as the concepts of virtue and justice, whose representation was allegorical.

Wordsworth famously describes the radical transformation of both art and artist. He chose as the object of art what he calls ordinary situations and men. Even more importantly, in his preface the artist takes on a new and more important role than ever before. In fact, the notion of the artist's special sensibility and extraordinary talent elaborated earlier by Kant and emphasized by Wordsworth would become one of the key features of Romanticism. Unlike in the Kantian elaboration of artistic genius, however, Wordsworth's description of the poet does not mystify the process of artistic creation. Wordsworth depicts that which has become a commonplace assumption about art ever since his Preface: namely, that the artist neither fully invents the fictional world he or she creates nor mirrors it exactly as is. Instead, artists and poets "throw over them [real people and events] a certain colouring of imagination, whereby ordinary things should be presented to the mind in an unusual way; and, further, and above all, to make these incidents and situations interesting by tracing in them, truly though not ostentatiously, the primary laws of our nature: chiefly as regards the manner in which we associate ideas in a state of excitement" (Preface, 392).

When art no longer serves the purpose of representing a world created by God and of conveying its meaning to others, the artist assumes a double nature. On the one hand, he's a created, fragile being in a world which appears to be forsaken by the divine. On the other hand, he's a creator of extraordinary beauty and true meaning. These paradoxical features would outlast the movement of

Romanticism. The (post)romantic artist is therefore both infinitely small and infinitely powerful; a finitude aspiring to the infinite. It's no accident then that critics who study Romanticism speak of a ladder of love similar to the one we find in Platonic thought, especially in the *Symposium*. Romantic artists, poets and writers select details from ordinary life and infuse them with special significance, beauty and meaning. As in Plato's transcendental moves, Romantic artists and writers begin with the particular—contingent events and human beings—and aspire to render them universal or, in Wordsworth's own formulation, "interesting by tracing in them... the primary laws of our nature" (392).

Through his talent, the artist manages to convert a flood of accidental details into something readers will find essential; into some kind of lasting meaning. Wordsworth seems aware, however, that to speak of conveying an "essential nature" and meaning through art risks converting aesthetics into a form of rational knowledge. Although the Romantic poet may strive to capture some kind of truth about the human condition, as we have already observed, he does not aim at a strictly mimetic truth (where art strives, imperfectly, to imitate the universe as created by the divine) nor at a strictly rational one (whereby art provides knowledge in the same way that mathematical proofs or scientific experiments do). Which is why Wordsworth hastens to add that the source of creativity is not reason, but rather passion. Artists at once discover and create what he calls "the primary laws of our nature" by cultivating an emotive disposition "chiefly as regards the manner in which we associate ideas in a state of excitement" (392).

Wordsworth places emotion at the very center of human creativity. He places value not upon raw and immediate reactions to concrete circumstances, however, but upon feelings recalled and evoked in moments of quiet contemplation. As the contemporary writer Jean Rouaud would later say by way of analogy, the (post)romantic artist is not the being creating natural flowers, but rather the florist arranging them in an elegant vase, contemplating their beauty calmly in light of its aesthetic arrangement of forms and potential impact to move and please viewers. With this analogy in mind, we're now ready to consider Wordsworth's famous definition of the poetic process:

> For all good poetry is the spontaneous overflow of powerful feelings but though this be true, poems to which any value can be attached, were never produced on any variety of subjects but by a man, who being possessed of more than usual organic sensibility, had also thought long and deeply. (393)

We have already noted that if Romantic poetry aims to convey some kind of essential truth, it's an anthropocentric one, not one that mirrors a divine vision and creation. Furthermore, we have observed that this truth differs substantially from scientific claims. So what is the nature of specifically aesthetic knowledge? And what is the process of its transmission and verification, if it eludes scientific and even rational scrutiny? Given the fragility of aesthetic knowledge, and, furthermore, given its anthropocentric nature, Wordsworth and other Romantic poets and writers would attempt to establish its tenuous foundations upon aesthetic sensibility. The foundation of art is the exceptional talent of the artist to convey beautifully and movingly essential aspects of the human condition. In turn, its only measure of success is the attunement it finds in generations of readers. For as Wordsworth suggests, the poet "shall describe objects, and utter sentiments, of such a nature and in such connection with each other, that the understanding of the being to whom we address ourselves, if he be in a healthful state of association, must necessarily be in some degree enlightened, and his affections ameliorated" (400).

Art's truth—and power—consists of its ability to capture a contingent meaning which may not be everlasting, but which touches us with its very contingency. This truth emerges, on the side of the artist, in a kind of séance that combines what may be called, before its time, subconscious thought and what Wordsworth calls processes of volition. For Romantic writers, the poetic process entails a creative recollection of one's own feelings "So that it will be the wish of the Poet to bring his feelings near to those of the persons whose feelings he describes, nay, for short spaces of time perhaps, to let himself slip into an entire delusion, and even confound and identify his own feelings with theirs; modifying only the language which is thus suggested to him, by a consideration that he describes for a particular purpose, that of giving pleasure"(400).

Aesthetic emotion, or what could also be called passion, connects every point on the route to artistic creation. An intense yet calm contemplation, the evocation of feelings, ignites the creative process. Through carefully selected words, the poet must be able to move readers, but once again not to raw emotions, but to aesthetic sensibilities that give both purposeless pleasure and a sense of meaning. The power of art, in turn, is tested only by time. It has no other true standard, for only the accumulated responses of readers can give it lasting value. But the question still remains: If Wordsworth aims at a contagion of aesthetic feelings and sensibilities from poet to readers through poetry, then why must he appeal to a higher, universal standard of truth? In other words, if the goal of art is emotive and aesthetic—to move through beauty—then why does he insist that the poet must express a human essence and meaning? The poet addresses this question by connecting Romantic art to truth, or, more generally, aesthetics to epistemology:

> Aristotle, I have been told, hath said, that Poetry is the most philosophic of all writing: it is so: its object is truth, not individual and local, but general, and operative; not standing upon external testimony, but carried alone into the heart by passion; truth which is its own testimony, which gives strength and divinity to the tribunal to which it appeals, and receives them from the same tribunal. Poetry is the image of man and nature (401).

As much as Wordsworth makes the power of Romantic art dependent upon the transmission of aesthetic emotion from real artist to real readers, he also wants to remove it from such sociohistorical contingencies by describing it as something that is measured by its own internal criteria and dependent upon nothing else. To do so, he depicts aesthetic truth in terms of the essence of the Romantic artist, a sensitive creator who captures "the beauty of the universe" and "the dignity of man" without any transcendental measure. He leaves us with a paradoxical vision of the artist which I call postromantic because we continue to find traces of it today: one aspiring to convey meaning without faith in either its objectivity or universality; one aspiring to move readers, but at the same time indifferent to the vicissitudes of their tastes; one which abandons the quest for an objectively verifiable truth only to engage in a process of intense contemplation of an elusive human essence which even the Romantic poet no longer fully believes exists.

Later Romantic writers and poets, including Charles Baudelaire, would realize how difficult it is to hold on to the epistemological rhetoric of truth when one is speaking of aesthetic beauty. For early Romanticism had presented more questions than it answered: In what ways can the truth of emotion and beauty be verified if not by generating a kind of consensus in viewers and readers? And even if, by a kind of magical Kantian subjective universal response, readers do indeed experience the same reaction to art and poetry, what does agreement have to do with truth? Can truth exist only in an anthropocentric context, without reference to higher standards? Couldn't human beings agree and still be wrong?

Sidestepping these problems, the late Romantic poet Charles Baudelaire returns art to the domain of aesthetics. Art, he suggests, is all about beauty, not truth. In the *Salon of 1846*, he declares:

> Each century, each people having possessed its own expression of beauty and morality – if we mean by Romanticism the most recent and modern expression of beauty – the great artist would therefore be –for the reasonable and passionate critic – the one that unites to the aforementioned condition, naiveté –the most Romanticism possible. (*Salon de 1846, Oeuvres Complètes*, 642).

So far it seems as if Baudelaire depicts beauty not as an attunement among author, text and implied reader, but rather as an attunement of poetry with its times. A work of art is one that best captures the feel of its epoch with elegance and pathos. The validation of art necessarily depends upon a social network of readers and critics who institutionalize that artistic perspective; who perceive it as in step with, and even ahead of, its times. Art is at once Romantic and modern, as Baudelaire puts it. While describing art as dependent upon the historical contingencies associated with artistic value, however, Baudelaire also agrees with earlier strands of Romanticism that the artist is the gifted creator of a timeless and abstract ideal:

> Romanticism lies neither in the choice of subjects nor in exact truth, but in the manner of feeling... For me, Romanticism is the most recent and up-to-date expression of beauty... The one who says Romanticism says modern art – which is to say intimacy, spirituality, color, aspiration towards the infinite – expressed by all the resources of art. (*Salon de 1846*)

Baudelaire thus returns to Wordsworth's image of the artist as a double figure: created in a world deprived of certainty; creator of beauty and meaning through art. External consecration does not suffice, however, to determine the quality of art. Like Wordsworth, Baudelaire is not fully prepared to abandon the artist to purely sociological standards. Hence his famous conception of art as doubled itself: as an intertwinement and juxtaposition of the ephemeral and the eternal; of passing fashion and timeless beauty:

> All forms of beauty contain, like all possible phenomena, something eternal and something ephemeral—the absolute and the particular. Absolute and eternal beauty doesn't exist, or rather it's nothing but an abstraction culled from the general surface of diverse forms of beauty. The particular element of each beauty comes from the passions, and as we have particular passions so we have our beauties. (*Salon de 1846*, 687)

In alluding to the eternal dimension of art, Baudelaire confronts the same problem as Wordsworth: by what standards can we judge an aesthetic object as eternal when we, ourselves, are only human; when the artist who created it, though perhaps more talented than ordinary human beings, is just as fallible and mortal as the rest of us? In "Notes nouvelles sur Edgar Poe," Baudelaire answers this question quite compellingly. He begins, like Wordsworth, by describing the creative origin and impact of poetry in a Platonic manner, as a "ravishment of the soul" (202). In other words, art is a process that transmits, by a kind of magical contagion or entrancement, the contemplation of passion rather than pure emotion itself. What is the aim of this aesthetic contagion? Nothing but the powerful feelings and impressions it provokes.

As we have seen, Baudelaire not only disassociates art from morality—as Wordsworth had in transforming the Neoclassical vision of art—but also from epistemology, or the discourse of truth. Poetry may make us more sensitive and sympathetic to other human beings, and it may even teach us something about human existence, but that is only incidental to it, not its central goal. "Poetry cannot," the author insists, "except at the price of death or decay, assume the mantle of science or morality; the pursuit of truth is not its aim, it has nothing outside itself" (204). So what is poetry then? Baudelaire responds:

> It's this admirable, this immortal instinct for Beauty that leads us to consider the earth and its spectacles as a correspondence with the Sky. The insatiable thirst for everything that is otherworldly and that reveals life is the living proof of our immortality. (*Notes nouvelles sur Edgar Poe*, 598).

Baudelaire's vision of poetry brings us to the threshold of what I call postromanticism: meaning a presentation of Romantic values and assumptions that remains plausible, and even intuitive, in modern times. Accepting the artist's double nature as creator of lasting beauty and created in a world without certainties, Baudelaire abandons the hope of proving the eternal value of art. Yet he still desires to claim it as an intuition, a hope. Baudelaire's modernist vision of Romanticism can be described as a powerful current that splits into two principal directions.

One direction would be pursued by Modernist and especially postmodernist artists and writers. This is the direction that postmodern theory has made most visible during the past thirty years. Beginning, as did Baudelaire, with the assumption that the beauty of art is not measured by any identifiable standard of truth or meaning, modernist and postmodernist authors would go so much further than the poet in dismantling --and showing the dangers of-- all traces of the universal from aesthetics. Once such criteria are removed, drawing qualitative distinctions among artistic objects and even between artistic and utilitarian objects becomes a matter of purely socioeconomic considerations. Thus we reach, as many maintain, the death of beauty and the end of art.

By way of contrast, what I call postromantic writers and artists take late Romantic assumptions similar to Baudelaire's to a different conclusion. If there's no higher measure of art's beauty and illumination, then the creative endeavor is all the more challenging, titillating and despairingly powerful. Postromantic poetry and art plausibly intertwine a passionate longing for the absolute with a sense of skepticism, and even hopelessness, towards the possibility of ever grasping it.

*Part 2*

# Postromanticism: The art of passion

Passion was the core of the Romantic movement and it is also, along with sensuality and the appreciation of beauty, the focal point of postromanticism. Sensuality and passion hardly seem separable since we tend to experience them together. It's nearly impossible to imagine passion without the excitement, agitation and upheaval of the senses and emotions that we associate with sensuality. At the same time, however, sensuality and passion are opposites. Sensuality is the acute sensibility to beauty and to the myriad of potential delights it promises. It's a way of seeing beauty in the world, in both human beings and objects. Such beauty is so vast and all-pervasive— *kalon*, or sea of beauty as Plato's prophetess, Diotima had depicted—that it's not necessarily anchored by any preference or bound by any attachment. Every week we may gaze at dozens of attractive persons, inspiring scenes and beautiful paintings or sculptures. Sensuality moves our eyes from object to object, stirring our desires, dreams and solipsistic emotions, but not necessarily capturing our devotion.

Much as sensuality, in its link to perception, evokes the aesthetic and epistemological dimensions of postromanticism, passion constitutes its ethics. This doesn't mean that postromanticism mandates that human beings should not appreciate a multitude of objects or beings. But it does unabashedly declare: love is special. Many of us fall passionately in love and such feelings are so miraculous that they seem to defy explanation. Yet, at the same time, they are so important that they have inspired thousands of writers, poets, philosophers and artists throughout human history to depict passionate love. Not everyone does or should fall deeply in love. But those who do, we tend to believe, are very fortunate. If passionate love is a privileged form of human experience that has intrigued us for millennia, then it's certainly worth valorizing it in our times.

Like Romanticism, postromanticism focuses above all on the expression of passionate love. Yet, in our day and age--an age so imbued with feminine and feminist sensibilities--one can no longer speak of the asymmetrical love between a male poet or artist and his ethereal muse, which has long been the dominant cliché of Romanticism. Postromantic love is reciprocal and symmetrical. Nor does postromanticism preserve the instrumental view of passion as a means of reaching something higher than human experience; of moving from the human to the divine, as we see in idealist traditions of love from Plato, to the Renaissance neoplatonists, to the Romantics. In Postromantic poetry, literature and art, passion begins with earthly existence and never transcends it.

*Definition:* So what is postromantic passion? Above all, passion is a focalization of the senses, thoughts and emotions upon one primary subject. I call it an ethics because it implies considering at every step one's attitude and actions towards the beloved and, conversely, his or her actions and feelings towards oneself.

*The transcendent in the contingent:* The beloved is not randomly chosen. Even if meeting him or her occurs by accident—as do most human encounters—the fit between the lovers feels so right that it appears to be determined by a higher force. The intervention of that higher force cannot be proven. Nonetheless, it has a certain metonymic logic similar to the one described by the Stoics, who perceived the imprint of divine will in the beauty and harmony of the universe. Postromanticism thus spiritualizes passionate love. It doesn't necessarily express a belief in divinity, but rather an elevation of emotion and human values. Passionate love is that which uplifts one's creative and life energies, as if by force of destiny, with the elegance, sense of wonder and inevitability of something that appears to transcend human experience.

*The artist and the muse:* With so many successful female artists in the world and, more generally, with so many women encouraged to pursue their talents, it's impossible nowadays to retain the Romantic idea of the artist as male and the muse as female. When the passion is shared, both members of the couple can inspire and engage in creativity.

*Idealization and lucidity:* While Romanticism tends towards the idealization of the beloved, postromanticism claims that the beauty of love and of the beloved often lies in his or her imperfection. For the Romantic poets the muse was otherworldly. Only through her nonexistence could she embody aesthetic ideals. She wasn't a woman, but a fantasy, a dream. In postromanticism, however, the source of inspiration is not a "crystallized" or idealized object of the imagination—as the novelist Stendhal had described love--but a contingent person who is known in the smallest details of his or her reality. Which is not to say that postromanticism follows the legacy of realism or naturalism. In postromanticism, unlike in naturalism, the mundane aspects of the lovers and of love itself never become scientifically predictable, mythical or grotesque, as they do, for instance, in Zola's naturalist fiction. Postromanticism declares: real love is endearing and unique; a product of a rare fit between two individuals who, through their mutual devotion, create lasting values in an ephemeral life.

***Focalization:*** We tend assume that the Romantic life is synonymous with the adventurous life, the life of an emotional tourist: traveling everywhere; having a multiplicity of relationships; experiencing each type of woman or man as one samples exotic dishes from distant parts of the world. Yet when one glides only on the surface of human existence, it's difficult to be immersed in passion. For passion requires time to become deeper, richer and more intimate; it requires focalization so that it will not disperse and become a flash of intensity that's one episode among a hundred others. In losing focus, passion also loses intensity and significance. It ceases to exist.

***Energy:*** Passion is a mutual consumption that gives rather than depleting energy. Like a windmill, like any rhythmic movement, it generates while absorbing energy, but not all by itself, but from the external impetus of two individuals' continual efforts to live for and with each other.

***Symmetry:*** Passion is constantly reinforced by symmetrical dialogue. The lovers negotiate everything and feel equal in the relationship. Which doesn't mean that they're identical. In fact, often passion becomes more exciting when the lovers share differences in temperament, point of view and opinion. Yet there are no conventional gender roles in postromanticism. One person is not necessarily more submissive, the other more authoritative; one person is not necessarily more emotive, the other more rational. The differences are unique to each couple, not necessarily polarized. They are diffused, varied and less predictable than in the Romantic complementarity between masculine and feminine roles.

***Reciprocity:*** Reciprocity, which was largely ignored by the Romantic movement, is the pillar of postromanticism. Passion that is mostly solipsistic— one human being's dream or projection upon an idealized person—is not real. It may represent desire or even a strong infatuation. But only once feelings, thoughts and desires are shared, do we enter the realm of passionate love.

***Proximity and distance:*** The Romantic male artists and their muses, even when they coupled in real life, appeared infinitely distant in art because the descriptions of women were so often veiled and disguised. The Romantics privileged the metaphors of woman as muse, angel, Salomé or *femme fatale*; of woman as all the more desirable because mysterious, multiple, changing and unattainable. In this tantalizing play and disguise of feminine identity, the difference between Romanticism, modernism and postmodernism is almost effaced. Postromanticism doesn't need feminine mystery and masquerade to cultivate desire and love. Which doesn't mean that it assumes love to be transparent. Postromanticism trusts that passionate love can generate its own dynamics: a constant movement between creating and lowering barriers which, unlike the Romantic vision of the *femme fatale* who fans desire through strategic advancements and withdrawals, is reciprocal, genuine and spontaneous.

**Breathing:** Passion is nourished by a proximity and intensity of communication so strong that it seems as if the lovers are breathing each other's air. Without suffocating. The withdrawals are themselves part of the process of breathing. They are periods of inhaling air, of absorbing life experience and knowledge, in order to exhale it back to one another; to have a renewed life energy to offer one's beloved.

**Thinking:** Postromantic passion is characterized by a rhythm and emotion which are genuine and spontaneous yet thoughtful at the same time. In this respect, it resembles Wordsworth's Romanticism, which described passion as a processed and thoughtful rather than immediate and visceral emotion. Without the mediation of thought, passion risks being just a passing fancy; a gust of wind. And winds quickly change direction. Passion is a symbiotic relation between two individuals who enable each other to interconnect the important aspects of human life, including sensation, emotion and thought. Passion engages all of our human faculties.

**Devotion:** Passion is an enduring devotion. It's not necessarily a commitment or responsibility in the way more institutionalized relations are, where the primary connection is external to the relationship. In other words, in passion the connection is not made by conventional morality and law. But the result is even more spectacular. Because devotion, a term evocative of religious experience, has transcendental connotations. Passion is a secular form of adoration.

**Fidelity:** We tend to believe that virtue is a more reliable foundation for fidelity than passion, but postromanticism says that's not the case. Virtue is often tested in the face of temptation and experienced as a tension between conscience and desire. All too often, the desire is more immediate, easier to satisfy and stronger. Passion reduces that tension and alleviates its pangs. In passion, the obsessive desire and focus upon a primary object is so strong that the energy left for others is weaker and more superficial, thus not posing a real threat to the relationship.

**Jealousy and Possessiveness:** If philosophers from Plato to Kant cautioned against passion, it's largely because they associated it with negative emotions such as jealousy, possessiveness and hatred, which occur when love turns full circle and collapses upon itself. The Romantics, from Goethe to Constant, often confirmed this negative impression in describing how the force of passion leads to madness, murder and suicide. It's undoubtedly true that passion is often accompanied by feelings of jealousy and possessiveness. Yet that's not necessarily a bad sign. In moderation, jealousy and possessiveness may constitute a declaration of love. They can express: I know you desire others and that others are desirable to me, but I need and am grateful for the uniqueness of our attraction and feelings. Jealousy, in moderation, rekindles the flame of passion. It suggests: out of all the desirable persons we meet, I still chose you and you me. In excess, however, jealousy snuffs out the flame of passion. It suggests: I don't trust you; you're not freely mine. Rather than loving you, I possess you.

***Ritual:*** Passion is a cherished ritual rather than a habit. A repetition of activities that appear to be always new, always exciting, because they're primarily motivated by emotions and desires. In lasting love, one needs the repetition of activities as one needs to breathe air or eat regularly, rather than going through the motions today out of inertia, because one did it yesterday. In its rhythm and intensity, the repetition of acts in passionate love—going to a movie, dining out--resembles the repetition of religious rituals.

***Erotism:*** Postromantic passion is erotic in a way that's intensely sensual and at the same time different from diffused sensuality. In passion, the physical longing for someone is stimulated by knowledge and love of that person, rather than the love being motivated primarily by desire. That's what makes passion different from the multiplicity of human attractions. While sensuality is a feast for the senses, passion offers food for the soul. Postromanticism places passion at its center, declaring: life and art would be emptier and more impoverished without such exquisite nourishment.

# Bibliography

Abrams, M. H. *The Mirror and the Lamp: Romantic Theory and the Critical Tradition*. Oxford: Oxford University Press, 1953.
Abrams, M. H. *Natrural Supernaturalism: Tradition and Revolution in Romantic Literature*. New York: W.W. Norton, 1971.
Allen, James Smith. *Popular French Romanticism: Authors, Readers, and Books in the Nineteenth Century*. Syracuse: Syracuse University Press, 1981.
Armstrong, Nancy. *Desire and Domestic Fiction: A Political History of the Novel*. Oxford: Oxford University Press, 1995.
Berlin, Isaiah. *The Roots of Romanticism*. Princeton: Princeton University Press, 1999.
Bloom, Harold. *The Western Canon: The Books and School of the Ages*. New York: Penguin Putnam, 1994.
Bloom, Harold. *Romanticism and Consciousness: Essays in Criticism*. New York: W.W. Norton, 1970.
Cavell, Stanley. *In Quest of the Ordinary: Lines of Skepticism and Romanticism*. Chicago: University of Chigaco Press, 1994.
Champigneulle, Bernard. *Rodin*. London: Thames and Hudson, 1999.
Clark, Kenneth. *Romantic Rebellion: Romantic Versus Classical Art*. New York: Galahad Books, 1977.
Danto, Arthur. *After the end of art: Contemporary art and the pale of history*. Princeton: Princeton University Press, 1997.
Danto, Arthur. *Encounters and reflections: Art in the historical present*. Berkeley: University of California Press, 1986.
Danto, Arthur. *The State of the Art*. New York: Prentice Hall Press, 1987.
Danto, Arthur. *The Transfiguration of the Commonplace: A Philosophy of Art*. Harvard: Harvard University Press, 1981.
Danto, Arthur. *The Philosophical Disenfranchisement of Art*. New York: Columbia University Press, 1986.
De Man, Paul. *The Rhetoric of Romanticism*. New York: Columbia University Press, 1984.
Descartes, René. *Les Passions de L'Ame*. Paris: Librairie Philosophique J. Vrin, 1991.

Descartes, René. *Correspondance avec Elisabeth et autres lettres*, Paris: G.F. Flammarion, 1989.
Diderot, Denis. *Oeuvres: Tome IV (Aesthetique)*. Edited by Laurent Versini. Paris: Robert Laffont, 1996.
Eldridge, Richard. *The Persistence of Romanticism*. Cambridge, Cambridge University Press, 2001.
France, Peter (Editor). *The New Oxford Companion to Literature in French*. Oxford: Clarendon Press, 1995.
Furst, Lilian R. *Romanticism*. London: Methuen and Co., 1969.
Furst, Lilian R. *Romanticism in perspective: A comparative study of aspects of the Romantic movements in England, France and Germany*. New York: Macmillan, 1969.
Furst, Lilian. *European Romanticism: Self-Definition, An Anthology*. New York: Routledge, 1980.
Gablik, Suzi. *Reenchantment of Art*. London: Thames and Hudson, 1992.
Gablik, Suzi. *Has Modernism Failed?* New York: W.W. Norton, 1985.
George, Albert Joseph. *The Development of French Romanticism: The Impact of the Industrial Revolution on Literature*. Syracuse: Syracuse University Press, 1955.
Goldstein, Car. *Teaching Art: Academies and Schools from Vasari to Albers*. Cambridge: Cambridge University Press, 1996.
Gombrich, E.H. *The Story of Art*. New York: Phaidon Press, 1950.
Halsted, John. B. (Editor). *Romanticism*. New York: Walker and Company, 1969.
Harth, Erica. *Cartesian women: Versions and Subversions of Rational Discourse in the Old Regime*. Ithaca: Cornell University Press, 1992.
Herold, Christopher. *Mistress to an Age: A life of Madame de Stäel*. New York: Grove Press, 1958.
Isbell, John. *The Birth of Romanticism: De Staël's De l'Allemagne*. Cambridge: Cambridge University Press, 1994.
Kenin, Richard. The Art of Drawing: From the dawn of history to the era of the Impressionists. New York: Paddington Press, 1974.
Lockridge, Laurence S. *The Ethics of Romanticism*. Cambridge: Cambridge University Press, 1989.
Majewski, Henri. *Transposing Art into Texts in French Romantic Literature*. North Carolina: University of North Carolina Press, 2002.
Nussbaum, Martha. *Upheavals of Thought: The Intelligence of Emotions*. Cambridge: Cambridge University Press, 2001.
Peyre, Henri. Translated by Roda P. Roberts. *What is Romanticism?* Alabama: University of Alabama Press, 1977
Richard, Jean-Pierre. *Littérature et Sensation*. Paris: Editions du Seuil, 1954.
Robinson, Jeffrey C. *The Current of Romantic Passion*. Madison: The University of Wisconsin Press, 1991.
Vaughan, William. *Romanticism and Art*. London: Thames and Hudson, 1994.

Vila, Anne. *Enlightenment and Pathology: Sensibility in the Literature and Medicine of Eighteenth-Century France*, Baltimore: Johns Hopkins University Press, 1998.
Wedberg, Anders. *A History of Philosophy: The Modern Age to Romanticism*. Oxford: Clarendon Press, 1985.
Wolfe, Tom. *The Painted Word*. New York: Bantam, 1975.
Wolfe, Tom. *From Bauhaus to our House*. Bantam, 1981.
Wordsworth, William. *Lyrical Ballads*, Edited by William Richey and Daniel Robinson. Boston: Houghton Mifflin Company, 2002.
Wu, Duncan (Editor). *A Companion to Romanticism*. London: Blackwell Press, 1999.

*Part 3*

# Postromantic poetry:
# The painful poignancy of desire

*by Claudia Moscovici*

*The book of life*

*Our changing moods leaf through my life*
*Like the wind sweeps through the pages of a book.*
*Sometimes I'm overwhelmed by emotion*
*And need you with the desperation of a child;*
*At others I live with you a gentle and untroubled love story*
*A slice of human existence frozen in time.*
*Sometimes the plot twists and turns*
*And I wreathe from the pain of jealousy and hate;*
*At other times the rhythmic waves of passion*
*Soothe everything and carry us away.*
*And when you close yourself with care and sadness*
*I open your being with the gentleness of my caress;*
*And when I burst in flames of madness*
*You shelter my fire with the cup of your hands.*
*Sometimes I feel that our story is over,*
*That the plot has nowhere left to go*
*But all I need is the touch of your finger*
*To perceive infinity in the book we are writing each day.*

*Blown away by the gentle breeze*

*Without seeking anyone, I found you upon my path*
*As a gratuitous gift from a fate that appeared haphazard and blind,*
*As a rare blessing in a life sheltered from the gaze of the divine.*
*Without feeling empty, you filled a void I thought I lacked*
*As an evanescent happiness that dissolves into an impossible dream,*
*As an inspiring illusion that traces the boundaries of everyday reality.*
*Without being lonely, I kept your distant company in mind*
*As an intimate closeness that intertwines parallel paths,*
*As a bond of freedom that attracts but never unites.*
*Without needing solace, I was moved by your intangible touch*
*As a gentle breeze that caresses the dark evening sky,*
*As the hurricane of emotions that has elevated my life.*

*My love, I will come to you tonight*

*My love, I will come to you tonight
To make waves of desire in the stillness of your sleep
Without causing a storm, without perturbing your dreams.
I will flow along the softness of your skin
As a summer wind, as a tranquil stream.
And my gift to you will be the light of the sun,
A prism of feelings with the power of song.
Since with you this brief moment we call human life
Is a chasm we cross in a thrilling flight.
And if in your sleep, you will fly with me,
I promise to love you and be true to thee;
To welcome you warmly with a burning heart;
To the infinite space of our mortal love.*

*You are everything*

*The waves of the sea envelop my being and carry me away*
*To a space where the tears of solitude join the sky of regret*
*And the passage of time becomes frozen in infinity.*
*In that space the pain of existence is effaced*
*By the gentle flow of each passing day.*
*You are the waves, you are the space, you are the sea.*

*The summer wind flirts with my skirt as I set sail on this lonely path*
*It makes me laugh all to myself as I remain alone and untouched.*
*I am surrounded by voices, by beings and glances,*
*By the push and pull of a hectic life,*
*Yet all I hear is the cries of my heart*
*Longing to join the silence of your touch.*
*You are the voice, you are the touch, you are the wind.*

*The burning sun closes my eyes to the flickering flame we call life*
*Making me wonder where each pulse of our hearts*
*And each breath will carry us*
*I follow that light like a blind woman moving through the tunnel of fate*
*Seeking to find a glimmer of hope, the illumination*
*Of meaning in those dark corridors*
*And there, I find you. You are the light, you are the hope, you are the sun.*

*The tide*

*I see the brightness of the sun in your adoring gaze*
*I feel the coolness of the sea in your light caress*
*I sense the softness of the breeze in your gentle face*
*You fill my soul with love and tenderness.*

*Your words make my heart echo and resonate*
*Your unique beauty can only surprise and inspire*
*Each phrase you utter, each thought you formulate*
*Attracts and repels me with simultaneous respect and desire.*

*You mold my body like a sculptor with your eager touch*
*You trace its contours with both palms and tongue*
*I moan with pleasure as I cry with pain; I feel so much*
*That you are the only melody that can accompany my song.*

*I am attuned to the gentle music of each breath you take*
*Your skin tantalizes my hands with its fragile softness*
*I dance to the slow rhythm of each move you make*
*As you fill and deplete my soul with the tide of happiness.*

*With and without you*

With you, I want to see the world in all of its resplendent hues
The summer greens, the vivid reds, the sunny yellows and the ocean blues.
I want to taste upon your lips the salty flavor of the sea
And as I delve into your waves, I wish to learn what it means to be.

And when you push me gently away so you can catch your breath
I want to feel the rhythm of life in the air you exhale.
And when I pull you back towards me until we move as one
I want to feel the warmth you give with the brightness of the sun.

And when you leave I want to feel your presence like a dream
A velvety voice, the ring of laughter, a smile I've barely seen.
I want to feel you rule my world even when we are apart
I want to know our separate lives pulsate in the same heart.

*When...*

*When the weight of the world comes crashing down on my shoulders,*
*When moments of sorrow chain together a pearly strand of tears,*
*When bad luck pursues me with the hunger of a starving wolf,*
*When I mourn and regret the day I never asked to be born,*
*I turn to you.*

*And with the strength of your friendship you lift the weight of the world,*
*And with the compassion of your desire you tell me I look beautiful in pearls,*
*And with the endurance of your loyalty you protect me from the twists of fate,*
*And with the fervor of your prayers you make me appreciate each day,*
*And with the power of your love you make me want to live again.*

*Siesta*

*When I hear the wind whistling through the trees*
*I think of the sunny breeze that soothed our tired bodies*
*That dried pearly beads from your glistening, soft skin*
*That, when you left, wiped away tears of loneliness and chagrin.*

*When I see the brightness of the shining sun*
*I think of the rays of hope that seeped through our blinds*
*That striped our sleep with the shadows of clouds*
*That illuminated our souls with the sparkle of life.*

*Evening prayer*

*Softness of dream*
*Gentle flow of stream*
*Twinkle of star*
*Wherever you are*
*Please hear my prayer*
*Whisper it to him*
*Wherever he may be*
*So far away from me*
*He hears my every breath*
*He listens to my steps*
*He looks for signs of me*
*He seeks me everywhere*
*Tell him I long for him*
*Tell him I dream of him*
*Tell him I feel his heart*
*Tell him we'll never part*

*Remember*

*My sweetheart, gentle lover*
*If you forget my name*
*When other waves of passion*
*Will carry you away*
*Remember all the echoes*
*Of footsteps when I came*
*Remember when you told me*
*You also felt the same*
*Remember the soft rhythm*
*The night you took my heart*
*Remember streams of tears*
*The day we had to part*

*Desire*

*Your glance moves through my tresses*
*Flows on my arms, softly grazes my skin.*
*My eyes sparkle with light, looking at you*
*I feel happy; I forget my chagrin.*

*Your lips barely caress my ears,*
*Whisper sweet nothings, who knows what you say.*
*My knees tremble with weakness*
*I melt in your arms; I feel carried away.*

*Your hands probe my whole being,*
*Finding its secrets, stirring its dreams.*
*I gasp with desire, seeking to find you,*
*To capture your body, to enfold you within.*

*Butterfly*

*Translucent wings, a kaleidoscope of color*
*Beating against the blueness of the sky*
*Gliding motion, barely can feel it*
*Making a feast of spring out of life.*

*Hazel eyes, the richest of colors*
*Flickering against the beat of my heart*
*Caressing motion, barely can feel it*
*Growing the spring of love in our lives.*

*My voyage*

*I sit on the shore, close my eyes and dream*
*Of the many voyages I could have taken in life*
*I could have traveled on the calmest of seas*
*To glide my way smoothly like a bird*
*I could have taken adventurous trips*
*To feel the thrill of every storm*
*I could have stopped in many towns*
*To take bright pictures that would soon look worn*
*I could have lived completely bound*
*Or could have boldly seized the day*
*Instead, I chose this middle ground*
*Of taking few risks yet making waves*
*Of being free yet needing trust*
*Of settling down in a single port*
*While in the vastness of the sky*
*Finding the freedom that I lost*

*To live*

*You ask, what does it mean to live?*
*Is life the slow struggle of an ant*
*Carrying with all its might a crumb*
*Or is it the last explosion of a star*
*Before darkness displaces light?*
*Is life the march towards a tomb*
*Where nothingness holds sway*
*Or is it a butterfly's easy flight,*
*The wondrous voyage of a day?*
*Is life the slow growth of a tree*
*Towards a dim source of light*
*Or is it plunging in a depth*
*That knows no touch or sight*

*Diamonds and pearls*

*You ask me why my tears flow*
*Full, round, one falling upon the other*
*Strung together like translucent pearls*
*Drops of emotion filled with generosity*
*Yet errant, overwhelming, capricious*
*Cupped by moist eyes and begging*
*To be consoled by trembling hands*
*Or kissed by soft, compassionate lips*
*In a quivering voice I give you my answer*
*Life's like a search of precious stones*
*Among the dull, nondescriptive pebbles*
*Strewn along our paths we find*
*Rare moments of pleasure and joy*
*Gleaming with the unmistakable intensity*
*Of diamonds that even retrospectively*
*Have density and endure the test of time*
*These are the only memories that count*
*What we experience here and now*
*These are the only moments we exist*
*The rest, my love, we merely live*

*A siren's song*

*I have risen, gentle lover*
*From the quiet depths of sea*
*To encircle you forever*
*Into me*

*My hair is the ocean's currents*
*My touch is the softest breeze*
*I excite the sweetest torments*
*That exist*

*My eyes sparkle in the moonlight*
*Glitter like the richest gems*
*Making everything seem bright*
*That you see*

*In my arms, forget the future*
*Let the past be but a dream*
*Let the second flow forever*
*Like a stream*

*And when you remember others*
*Let the music of my song*
*Soothe away your deepest troubles*
*Nothing's wrong*

*Let my body be your treasure*
*Let your sorrow be our prayer*
*Forget every rule and measure*
*Have no care*

*Klimt's women*

*Elongated, sinuous forms, golden leafs*
*Pressed between quivering lips*
*Caressed by the fugue of your fingertips*
*Kissed by the intangible touch*
*Of eyes filled with insatiable desire*
*Thousands of eager sirens can't*
*Quench the thirst of your parched needs*
*Their elusive, tempting, slippery bodies*
*Glide silently into all of your dreams*
*As waves of emotion moisten*
*Only for a brief, fugitive moment*
*The inconsolable loneliness you feel*

*Dream*

*Eyes sparkling deep*
*Lightest of sleep*
*Mouth full of kisses*
*All that I'm missing*
*Hands that explore*
*Lips that adore*
*Don't hesitate*
*Forget your regret*
*Delve into me*
*Swim in my sea*
*Ride on my waves*
*Find all enclaves*
*Richest of life*
*Passion and strife*
*Full of emotion*
*To and fro motion*
*Flow like a stream*
*Color my dream*
*Show me desire*
*Lift me up higher*
*Take my breath away*
*With your gentle sway*
*Give me a pleasure*
*Beyond all measure*
*Shine from afar*
*Explode like a star*

*Your hometown*

*Bring me to your youthful past*
*To old memories, hidden desires*
*Like a hot and luminous fire*
*Sheds new light upon a familiar home.*
*Lay me down upon your memories*
*Gently, as upon a bed of flowers*
*Let our present love reveal*
*Every moment's hidden powers.*
*And when you will feel tempted*
*To live only in the past*
*Twirling softly, cradling gently*
*Former lovers in your arms,*
*Let the shower of my kisses*
*Wake you up from former flings*
*Let us toast the days we're missing*
*Celebrating our new dreams.*

*Stronger*

*I know the force of habit*
*That makes each day seem the same*
*I sensed the sweet temptation*
*Of lovers without name*
*I felt the harsh indifference*
*Shower the coldness of fall rain*
*I have sensed time and distance*
*Lay memories to shame*
*I know the power of hatred*
*To destroy all the past*
*And to transform each memory*
*Into a regretful farce*
*But I promise you sincerely*
*In the name of all I love*
*That our feelings are stronger*
*Than everything I know*

*Cocoon*

*Underneath the soft folds*
*Protected from light*
*Protected from sight*
*I awake to new life*
*Through closed eyes I perceive*
*The darkness of warmth*
*The contours of dream*
*The scent that I know*
*The velvet I touch*
*The rhythm I feel*
*The comfort you give*
*The strength that I take*
*From that nourishing flow*
*Evanescent fantasies*
*Condense as emotions*
*In a torrent of passion*
*With moist lips I explore*
*The flower that grows*
*From the seed of our love*

*Patience versus Tolerance*

*Your indulgent smile, mixed with my tears*
*Makes me feel like a child burdened with years*
*You tease my emotions; you ease all my pain*
*And when you comfort me gently, you put me to shame.*

*Not a word of impatience; not a moment's indifference;*
*Not a stroke of rejection, and that makes all the difference.*
*For I never want the shadow of tolerance, with its cold rationality*
*To displace your warm patience, and its light conviviality.*

*Traces of you*

*I trace the contours of your being upon the folds of life*
*I wrap you up into myself to stop the flight of time*
*I count the years and save each day we leave behind*
*You are the treasure I will cherish until the day I die*

*I see the gleam of happiness in your tired eyes*
*I close the blinds so only you can be my source of light*
*And in the dark when I'm alone I climb upon your rays*
*You are the sunlight I will seek until the end of my days*

*Invitation*

*Concentric circles of expanding emotion*
*Fluttering wings of butterflies in motion*
*Light breath hastened by excitement*
*Trembling hands eager to find you*
*Soft body seeking your touch*
*Fine hair leaving waves in the sand*
*Warm lips melt your shyness away*
*Tears of love invite you to stay*

*Whispers*

*I count the pearly strands of tears*
*One by one, until I lose sight of myself*
*Wondering in the chasm between dream and reality*
*I see you beautiful and strong*
*You wrap yourself around me*
*To protect me from the world*
*You envelop me softly, warmly*
*In the folds of your fragility*
*My fingers barely dare to touch your skin*
*As I whisper those familiar words in your ear*
*You listen to the sound of my breath*
*As it tickles you with its gentle heat*
*And you feel moved no matter what I say*
*Because you know from the warmth*
*Of that touch, of that sound, how I feel*

*Timidity*

*I like the way you barely look at me sometimes,*
*Stealing a glance, obliquely, like a voyeur.*
*The way your furtive touch brushes my skin*
*Tantalizingly soft, withdrawing, timid.*

*I like the way you give yourself away*
*By wrapping your emotions like a gift*
*I open you with the slightest touch*
*I take you in, enfold you, breathe you.*

*I like the way you try to avoid our pain*
*By making light of it, through diversions, singing,*
*The way it clings to us from time to time anyway*
*Light as a cloud, disorienting, feeling.*

*Writing love*

*Dip your pen in the pool of my glance*
*Find within me the ink of our feelings*
*Punctuate with kisses the end of each stance*
*Leave questions to those who seek meaning*
*Trace gently the contours of my face*
*With metaphors as soft as a whisper*
*Let imperatives determine the pace*
*And the turns of the dance we will follow*
*Twirl gently loose strands of my hair*
*Wrap my body in long phrases, rich symbols*
*Let your feelings flow through your words*
*Sign your name in the folds of my being*

*Falling leaves*

*Leaves glittering in the sun*
*Fall upon me lightly, gently*
*A fire without warmth;*
*A life that is already dead.*
*They wink; they sparkle*
*Deceptively, as a palette of colors*
*Cheerfully sprinkles the earth*
*Only to be trampled upon;*
*To lose color and wholeness*
*Leaving no trace except*
*For the soft, inaudible, whisper*
*Of leaves decomposing in the night.*

*Today*

*You try to recall*
*Traces of your past*
*Idealized moments*
*Hazy, effervescent, soft*
*They fall light as dew*
*Upon your tired eyes*
*The tears I see in you*
*Glitter inside my heart*
*They give a glow to life*
*To youth, to days forever gone*
*To time itself, to our helplessness*
*Before its rapid fugue*
*An innocent kiss*
*The sense of wonder*
*The fluttering of your mind*
*They seem but distant visions*
*And figments lost in time*
*Yet as I dry your tears*
*By wiping my own eyes*
*I face our nostalgic mirror*
*With reflections about today*
*For I perceive so clearly*
*In your mesmerizing gaze*
*In the beauty of our present*
*Tomorrow's yesterday*

*Ataraxia and passion*

*The first thing you ever told me*
*Was that you wanted inner peace*
*Ataraxia, a life in balance*
*The freedom from external disturbance*
*That induces pleasure and contemplation*
*In short, the life of a philosopher king*
*I still had tears in my puzzled eyes when*
*You talked about tranquility*
*And my body was nervously shaking*
*From a recent tantrum*
*Which I just threw like a little girl*
*Agitated, anxious, whose desires*
*Are perpetually frustrated*
*Yet the glimmer in your eyes*
*And your amused smile*
*Were somehow infectious to me*
*They elevated my spirits*
*As your tender voice took over*
*Soothing my deepest fears*
*Swooping me off my feet*
*From the brink of the chasm*
*Which, you showed me*
*So lovingly, didn't even exist*

*From a distance*

*I wish I could warm your body*
*With the soothing heat of my breath*
*And dissipate all your worries*
*With the softness of open hands*

*I wish I could show you emotion*
*With a single, fugitive glance*
*And capture your lifelong devotion*
*With the intimacy of my voice*

*I hope you can still feel my absence*
*In the warm trace I left on your bed*
*My form made room for your presence*
*In our memories you can find our embrace*

*I need you*

*I need you like the moon needs sunlight*
*To glimmer with hope in the night*
*I need you like the sky needs starshine*
*To sparkle with beauty and light*

*Yes, the moon could exist without sunlight*
*Invisible, lonely and old*
*As the sky could exist without starshine*
*Somber, brooding and cold*

*Holding hands*

*When you placed your little hand in mine*
*I understood that gesture meant unity and protection*
*And found sustenance and shelter in your gentle touch*
*As our fingers interlaced, separated, grasped*
*My moist palm grazed the softness of your skin*
*Then I lifted my arm to bring your hand to my lips*
*And that chaste, reverent kiss was my sacred vow*
*To support, respect, cherish and uplift you tomorrow*
*As much as I need, love and desire you today*

*Roots and air*

*The morning dew*
*Sparkles upon my finger*
*A treasure of emotion*
*I only need from you*
*The richness of desire*
*Warms up cooler evenings*
*And nights that tremble softly*
*In the briskness of the air*
*Sometimes when you're asleep*
*I extend my body upwards*
*Drawn by the luminous magic*
*Of stars that silently tempt me*
*With their majestic height*
*I bend, turn, stretch, move*
*With the smooth suppleness*
*Of a vine faithfully winding*
*Around her loyal trunk*
*You plant yourself in me*
*In you I find my shelter*
*From life's harshest storms*
*In the disarming intimacy*
*Of our communication*
*We find each other's roots*
*While breathing the fresh air*

*Adoration*

*Love is only the shadow*
*Of the emotions I feel*
*Vividly, tangibly, rippling*
*Through my tender skin*
*Making me shiver in the blaze*
*Of the summer heat*
*As a breeze plays with my hair*
*Embracing and caressing me*
*With memories of your touch*
*Light, titillating, promising*
*A timeless moment that extends*
*Towards an eternity we can almost glimpse*
*Shinning warmly, generously*
*Through the rays of the sun*

*Magic*

*You sorcerer, you dream*
*Your magic wand*
*Casts its spell over me*
*My eyes mesmerized*
*By your clement force*
*A drop of emotion on the tip*
*Beckons my tongue*
*To efface traces of love*
*To savor them with the fervor*
*Of the disorienting desire*
*You command through*
*The vulnerability and strength*
*Of the pleasure you give*

*Sleeping*

*Your body conforms to my shape*
*Sinuous, soft, protecting*
*Each other with a sleepy hand*
*Resting absentmindedly*
*Upon the hollow of a receptive waist*
*My hair flowing beneath your cheek*
*Tell me, my love, who needs a pillow*
*When my whole being enfolds you*
*With the cool lightness of silk*

*Life*

*When your tongue seeks the truth of my lips*
*A ventriloquism of pleasure escapes me*
*All I can do is moan softly, eyes shut*
*With a pleasure that overwhelms me*
*Which I hold deeply in my being*
*Afraid to let you go, to remain alone*
*Deprived of this solace of feeling*
*With you, the external world disappears*
*In the womb of my receptive body*
*Time flows only through our veins*
*Rapidly, feverishly, yet suspended*
*By the slow-motion of caresses*
*Your hand touching my skin*
*My lips repeatedly avowing emotion*
*Fervent kisses are only measure we need*
*To perceive the flow of our mortality*
*As a moment suspended, forgotten*
*In a life where nothing but love matters*

*Snowflakes*

*Our dance is the falling of snowflakes*
*An orderly yet irregular flight*
*A whirlwind of scattered emotions*
*Tempestuous, moving and light*

*As crystals, we cling to each other*
*Lost in the whiteness of space*
*We melt in the warmth of our passion*
*Only to take on a new shape*

*Snow*

*Falling snowflakes*
*Jewels of nature*
*Cling with hope*
*To our windowpane*
*Whiteness sparkles*
*Refracts color*
*Coldness meets*
*The warmth we share*
*As I watch this*
*Frantic motion*
*I take comfort*
*In your calm*
*And I lay beside you*
*Gently, softly*
*Not disturbing your repose*
*Indolent, peaceful and sleepy*
*I sense absent-minded hands*
*Seeking, stroking, even teasing*
*The soft landscape that is yours*

*Our quarrels*

*You feel puzzled*
*By these sudden eruptions*
*Of anger clouding blue skies*
*Rainstorms coming from nowhere*
*Trembling hands covering tearful eyes*
*You protest, you advance, you recoil*
*Your movements get lost in the sweep*
*Of fronts made of clashing desires*
*Of the soft consolations I seek*
*You approach to offer us shelter*
*From the roughness of summer storms*
*Cupped hands hold the flow of emotions*
*Gentle kisses stop the torrent of words*

*My voyage to you*

*Delicate lips*
*Quivering under*
*My touch*
*The moistness I seek*
*Embraces me*
*Inviting and warm*
*Flickering tongue*
*Absorbed in the*
*Hollow of mouth*
*Lapping the shores*
*Of these lands*
*Made for love*
*I let the flow*
*And the movement*
*Of your breath*
*Warm up my life*
*As wondering hands*
*Explore on their own*
*Adored and familiar sites*

*Contentment*

*Eyes nearly closed*
*Spying on the light*
*Seeping through the blinds*
*A streamlet of pleasure*
*Moves through me*
*While my body rests*
*Passively, timelessly, undisturbed*
*When the world stands still*
*Caught between our souls*
*Warmth, coziness, closeness*
*A disorienting dizzy spell*
*Of the peaceful euphoria*
*That only happens*
*When I nestle between you*
*And the rest of the universe*

*Erosion*

*We let playful waves*
*Lap over us happily,*
*Hungrily, carelessly.*
*The tide, we thought,*
*Can do us no harm.*
*We said to ourselves:*
*It will only clean us*
*And smooth out*
*All those rough edges:*
*We'll seem presentable*
*For once in our lives.*
*So the lukewarm water*
*Flowed between us*
*Soothing the sense*
*Of solitude and regret.*
*And it stripped us naked*
*Of our fierce needs*
*Of that mutual hunger*
*Which had been,*
*As we noticed later,*
*Our last self-defense.*
*Water came between us*
*Polishing our feelings*
*Into some unrecognizable*
*Form of politeness:*
*Strangers in this house.*
*We touch, we coexist*
*As an irreversible distance*
*Preserves and perfects*
*The erosion of feelings*
*We used to call love.*

*Undying love*

*I can face the coldness*
*Of a disconsolate future*
*Fraught with uncertainty*
*And dissipated dreams*
*As long as the fugue*
*Of your voice every morning*
*Chases away all my doubts*
*I can face the harshness*
*Of illness and weather*
*The unforgiving ravage of time*
*As long as the mirror*
*Of your eyes will still show me*
*Reflections of undying love*

*Nostalgia*

*A famous author once said
That once love is lost
You don't miss it
But you still can feel
Fading echoes, apathy
A persistent hollowness inside
When capricious memories
Tempt you to recall
The receding happiness
Which was once your existence*

*Pain*

*Eyes swollen shut*
*By the flow of tears*
*Out of my control*
*Rolling on their own*
*Down to the lump*
*Blocked in my neck*
*Even my breathing*
*Seems to stop expelled*
*By hiccups of pain*
*By tremors of shame*
*Ventriloquating pale lips*
*Slow-moving hips*
*Sway with emotion*
*In a prayer-like motion*
*The heaving chest*
*Pierced by stabs*
*It makes me scream*
*I want out of this dream*
*But the knife just thrusts*
*Till something inside bursts*
*As hands lost with despair*
*Pull and tug at my hair*

*The only way I like distance*

*The only way I like distance*
*Is protected by your gentle hand*
*When it cups my little breast*
*Giving me nourishment and life*
*Then my eyes can wonder*
*Past the soft blur of your face*
*Pressed so close to mine*
*That I can barely see you*
*And as my lips cling hopefully*
*To the sweetness of your mouth*
*My gaze flows, fading*
*Blissfully into the distance*

*The only way I like distance*
*Is enchanted by your velvet voice*
*When it soothes my ear*
*With its unbearable whispers*
*Then my mind can wonder*
*Past the softness of your tone*
*Brushing my cheek so warmly*
*That I can barely hear you*
*And as my heart beats wildly*
*To each word you say*
*I contemplate abstractly*
*The virtues of distance*

*The sweetness of your words*

*Give me the sweetness of your words*
*With the tip of your tongue*
*Let them glide into my mouth*
*Smoothly, wetly, generously*
*Let me savor the flavor of your thought*
*In the tingles that run through my being*
*In the feelings that condense into tears*
*Unarticulated, overwhelming, dense*
*Molecules of emotion too large*
*To flow through the pores of my skin*
*Pent up inside, but ready to burst*
*At your most delicate touch*
*At a barely whispered word*
*Into an unbearable surge of desire*
*Into the secret poetry that only*
*Our two bodies strained with the effort*
*Of an almost forgotten, soothing motion*
*That suckles the honey, the milk, and the spirit*
*From the sweetness of your words*

*Butterflies and flowers*

*Your voice flows through me*
*Tingles my skin; a warm bath*
*For the senses; a breeze of emotion*
*Unabashed gusts of pleasure*
*Move from you to me, from me to you*
*My eyes moisten from the life you impart*
*Effortlessly, with every word, with every gesture*
*In millions of little, thoughtless ways*
*Your being scatters like butterflies*
*That gather only to pollinate my being*
*And my petals open forever*
*To savor a single day of your love*

*Flurries*

*A flurry of memories*
*Cling to my soul*
*The taste of your lips*
*Is still on my tongue*
*The trace of your hand*
*Still pulls me close*
*The look in your eyes*
*Still unravels my mind*
*The feel of your cheek*
*Still makes me blush*
*As your mouth,*
*Sweet but hungry*
*Consumes me*
*Possesses me entirely*
*I'm all yours*
*When your lovely hands*
*Roam all over my body*
*Disheveling my hair*
*Titillating my skin*
*Inviting my touch*
*Probing my secrets*
*Until oh my love*
*I have nothing to hide*

*Waiting for you*

*Cars, blinking headlights*
*You could be anywhere*
*In any car, on any train*
*In any city, on any road*
*Everywhere and nowhere*
*I can't place you*
*I can't hold on to you at all*
*Yet none of that matters*
*Because you and I, my love*
*Breathe underneath*
*The same sky, sharing*
*Its dark blanket in the night*
*Cuddling together*
*In the warmth of half-dreams*
*In the heat of unfulfillable desires*
*As our emotions reawaken*
*Twinkling, flashing, beckoning*
*To those lonely stars in the night*
*In secret empathy with*
*The vastness of the sky*
*As fugitive feelings race by*
*I can barely perceive them*
*Out of the corner of my heart*
*When I await you every second*
*Impatient, excited, eager*
*And breathlessly in love*

*Insatiable*

*Your absence titillates me*
*With the impact of a desert storm*
*I retain the moisture you impart in a kiss*
*For months on end I survive*
*Alone, without the nourishment*
*Of your life-giving touch*
*My ears strain to hear the echo of your voice*
*My body's filled with the weight of our memories*
*I'm shivering for the warmth of your skin*
*I'm yearning for the smoothness of your touch*
*I'm starving for the food of your lips*
*I'm thirsty for the flow of emotion*
*I need you with a constancy*
*That touches upon religious fervor*
*I love you inexorably; I love you insatiably*

*The genealogy of my desire*

*You are, first of all, my brother*
*My protector, my family*
*I knew your every gesture*
*Long before we met*
*Every word rings familiar*
*A page ripped from my childhood*
*An album of family pictures*
*Evocations from a past*
*I can barely recall*
*That glows alive, movingly, in you*
*You are, above all, my partner*
*The one who dances with me*
*Each step of the way*
*Twirling my daily thoughts*
*Giving them movement, excitement*
*Conforming to my needs*
*Sometimes stepping on my feet*
*But never intentionally*
*Just with that adorable awkwardness*
*Which is a prelude to a kiss*
*You are my best friend as well*
*The one I confide in about everything*
*The one I need most, especially when*
*My brother and lover are too busy*
*To listen or care: it's then*
*That you, my sweetest friend*
*Are always there*

*Subtle emotions*

*My heart quivers*
*But ever so gently*
*With the tremor of*
*Agitated dreams*
*My eyes wonder*
*But only so slightly*
*Disoriented*
*By the intuitions I feel*
*Your soft voice*
*Ended abruptly*
*Echoing in the phone*
*I still held*
*And your goodbye*
*Oh so politely*
*Sent a chill*
*Through the warmth*
*Of our love*

*In your absence*

*In your absence, I break into fragments*
*More fragile than a porcelain figurine*
*I shatter from the impact of emotions*
*And so become a hand you held*
*The shirt I wore when you last touched me*
*The lips you kissed, the mouth you probed*
*Breathing life into me with your warmth*
*In your absence, I dissipate into the air*
*Lighter than any cloud, my thoughts*
*Float freely, detached from any anchor*
*They seek to reach you somewhere*
*Anywhere I may behold you again*
*In our past, in the present you travel*
*Without me, in the distant future*
*That I cannot fathom in your absence*

*Conversation*

*Your voice trickles like a stream*
*Drop by drop, word by word*
*Our intimate whispers condense*
*Into disoriented tear drops*
*Tracing zigzag patterns*
*Upon the velvet of our skins*
*Warm limbs cling together*
*Interlocked in clashing emotions*
*Pushed and pulled by waves of desire*
*Then soothed by those phrases*
*Which roll off our tongues*
*To moisten quivering lips*
*Provoking a delirium of pleasure*
*For what are lovers' vows*
*If not incantations filled with ecstasy*

*Illness*

*All-consuming warmth*
*Closed eyes burn*
*Emanating red sparks*
*Through wet eyelashes*
*In the heat of the summer*
*My body shivers with cold*
*Prodded by aches in muscles*
*I never even knew existed*
*As my mind, despite its spasms*
*Finds tranquility*
*In a semi-vegetative state*
*The signs of personality*
*Trickle out with the sweat*
*I'm bereft of my thoughts*
*But not of feelings*
*For now I'm pure sentient being*
*Tears cooling my cheeks*
*As I hear your soothing voice*
*Reassure me with sparse words*
*As your eloquent, worried silence*
*Tells me that in my sufferings*
*As in my joys, I'm never alone*

*Your voice*

The sound of your voice
Tickles temptingly, rolls smoothly
Inside of me, gliding instantly everywhere.
No echoes, no reverberations:
Just a simple hello.
A sound as clear as a bell,
As sharp as a whistle
And, as you know so well,
I'm instantly yours.
For it is as clear as day
That simple greetings
Unleash more complex emotions
Ravaging the folds of intimate memories;
Calling to mind Pavlov's dog.
What's up? you ask,
Almost matter-of-factly
And the fact is, my love,
That I need to catch my breath
If only to reply, nothing new,
Followed by the non sequitur:
If you knew how much I miss you…
Whispered with relief in the breath I exhale
What else is new… you ask ironically
While still caressing me with your tone
And with that indulgent, protective emotion
You withdraw; you advance; you cling to me
Then, overflowing, you fill me with your world.

*Fingerprints*

*You sometimes tease me*
*Saying that all I care about is pleasure*
*With me, there's not a sound without a touch*
*Always holding, caressing, enfolding, kissing*
*Sighing, moaning, needing, giving*
*I'm a hopeless sensualist*
*You claim, indulgently stroking my cheek*
*As tears glide down my face upon your fingers*
*For despite your caring gesture*
*I feel so hurt by your words*
*How mistaken you are!*
*Are we strangers, my love?*
*Don't you see that the pools of my eyes*
*Always mirror so intimately*
*Your handsome reflection?*
*I carry you in miniature everywhere*
*But you are greater than all of my desires*
*When we unite, feelings and pleasure*
*Are one, each implying the other*
*Yet as the latter passes, the former still remains*
*Oh, how can I explain? Perhaps like this:*
*Our love's the touch of moist, warm fingers*
*Leaving unique imprints of emotion*
*Upon the coolness of life's windowpane*

*Your dictionary*

*You ask, what is a touch?*
*I say, under your touch*
*I seem to take a more definite shape*
*My skin shivers smoothly*
*From a single gliding gesture*
*That leaves a trail of memories*
*Upon my sentient arm.*
*You ask, what is a kiss?*
*Well, it's only when we kiss*
*That I really know I have lips*
*And that somehow, mysteriously,*
*They transmit little bursts of happiness*
*To every part of my body*
*So that even my toes*
*Wiggle with glee when we kiss.*
*You ask, how much can words count?*
*Since I talk so much, I'm obliged to admit*
*That it would be quite embarrassing*
*To count words. But the truth, my love,*
*Is that words are priceless*
*For in sharing with you the minutia of my days*
*Each event glows with significance*
*So that without you the words*
*"Touch," "kiss" and "speak"*
*Would feel almost meaningless.*

***Delirious feelings***

***Glistening skin***
***Glows hauntingly white***
***Gliding motion***
***Eases the turmoil inside***
***Smooth curves flow***
***To shelter you in their cusp***
***An upheaval of waves***
***Bursts to cool feverish minds***
***Heat touching cold***
***Soothes all sensation of pain***
***Probing hands know***
***Silently just what to say***

*When you whisper what you want*

*When you desire something*
*You don't need to rile yourself up*
*Poised for battle, ready to crush*
*My needs with the force of your will*
*Why treat me like an enemy*
*When I'm your closest friend*
*Your partner, your life*
*The one who's on your side*
*Even when I seem to be on mine*
*For love has many facets*
*But, like a circle, it swirls around*
*To show seamlessly only one*
*So sweetheart, tell me what you want*
*Not with shouts or defensive gestures*
*Nor with commands I'm too proud to obey*
*But softly, gently, in barely audible whispers*
*Like a wish upon a star*
*Like a quiet incantation*
*That joins my silent need*
*To meet you half-way*
*To move as you move*
*To fulfill all your dreams*
*To protect you from harm*
*When you trust in my love*
*When you whisper what you want*

*Honeysuckle in the spring*

*When I was a little girl*
*My favorite season was spring*
*The breeze brushed*
*With its flowery scents*
*The dew off my skin*
*And my face bloomed*
*With an irrepressible smile*
*As I ran, greeting the wind*
*With all the joy I could express*
*Through the flowing*
*Uninhibited movements of my body*
*Out of breath, exhilarated*
*I would stop to touch the flowers*
*Breathing them through closed eyes*
*Bending over my favorite ones*
*Those little white stars*
*Twinkling among leafy ivy*
*Whose nectar I would suckle*
*Gently, smoothly, furtively*
*Pressing them between my lips*
*Savoring like a forbidden pleasure*
*The unforgettable taste, scent, feel*
*Of honeysuckle in the spring*
*That now, my love, only you can bring*

*The shadow of your shadow*

*Poetry is a Platonic cave*
*A wall of images*
*That captivate the imagination*
*To intensify emotions*
*One never thought one had*
*Or awaken those that lay dormant*
*In the tomb of a nearly forgotten past*
*To which no path returns*
*Innocently, you move about my world*
*Your life mirrored in these anonymous words*
*That pursue you with the intensity*
*Of a current I can't fully control*
*Which overwhelms me as much as it surprises you*
*So much so that to soothe this beautiful pain*
*I erect this wall of images that chant*
*An uplifting symphony of prayers*
*This shadow of your shadow*
*Is my elegy to love*

*To the very last*

*I'm just a tiny leaf*
*Trembling in the wind*
*Small, brittle, and frail*
*The brisk autumn air*
*Whistles through me*
*Moves me, mourns me*
*With its last love song*
*Viscous tears of amber*
*Glow around me, sparkle*
*Recalling the warmth*
*The light and the fire*
*Of seasons forever lost*
*With my tiny stem*
*Bending in the rain*
*I cling to your branch*
*My life, my only love*
*To the very last*

# About the Author

Claudia Moscovici is the author of five scholarly books on Enlightenment political philosophy and the Romantic movement, which include *Gender and Citizenship* (Rowman and Littlefield, 2000) and *Double Dialectics* (Rowman and Littlefield, 2002). She teaches philosophy, literature and arts and ideas at the University of Michigan in Ann Arbor. She has published poetry, short stories and essays in several literary magazines, including *Portland Magazine, Enigma Magazine, The Palo Alto Review, The Fairfield Review, WINGS, Outsider Ink, Nanny Fay Poetry Magazine, The Poetic Matrix, Three Cup Morning, Soul Fountain, Slate and Style* and *Möbius*.